ITS
ACCRUAL
WORLD

A COLORING BOOK FOR
ACCOUNTANTS

WHAT DO YOU CALL
AN ACCOUNTANT
WITHOUT A
SPREADSHEET?

LOST!

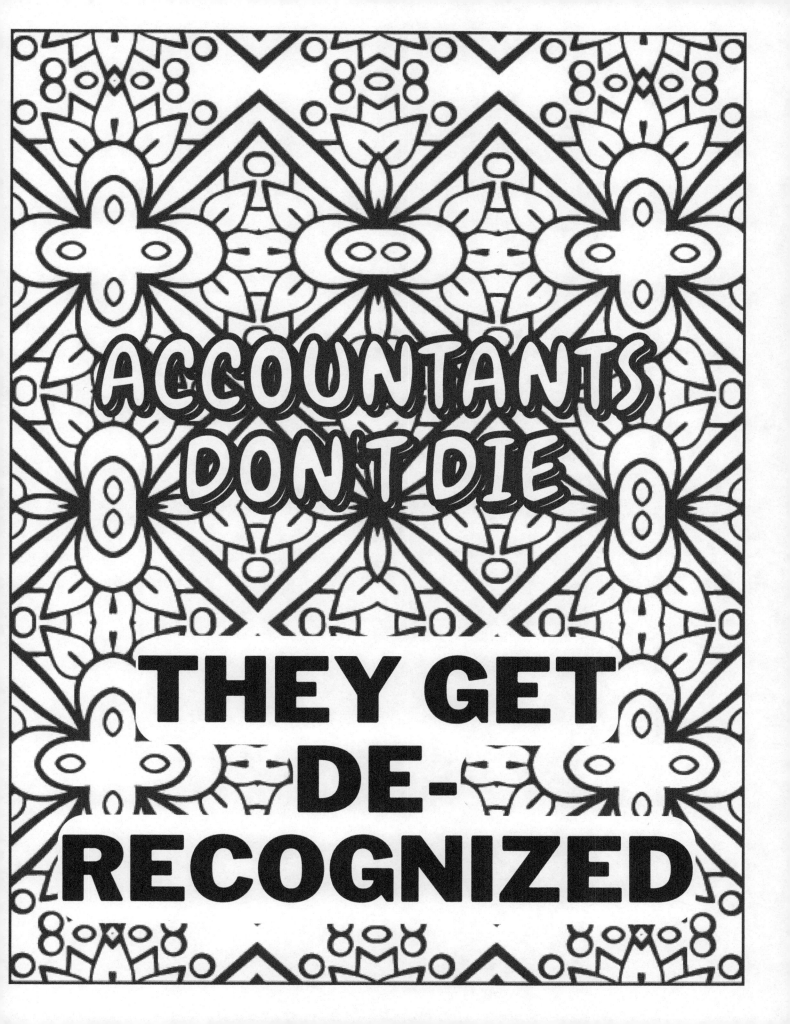

ACCOUNTANT
COUNCIL

THEY GET
DETECT
RECOGIZED

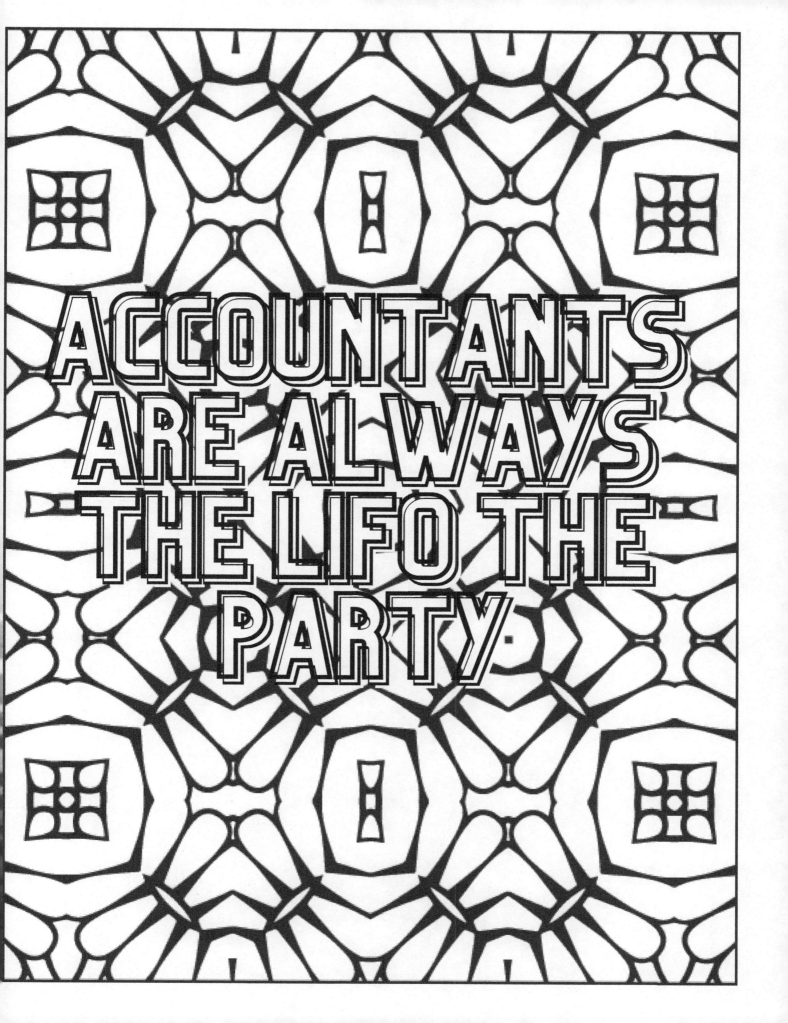

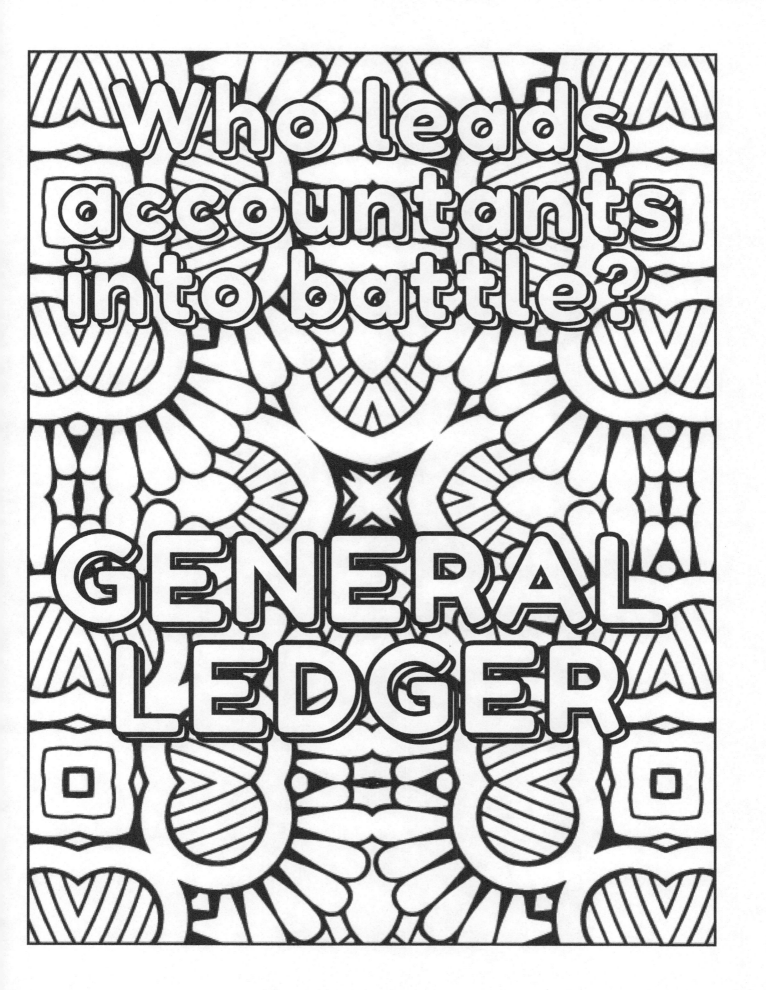

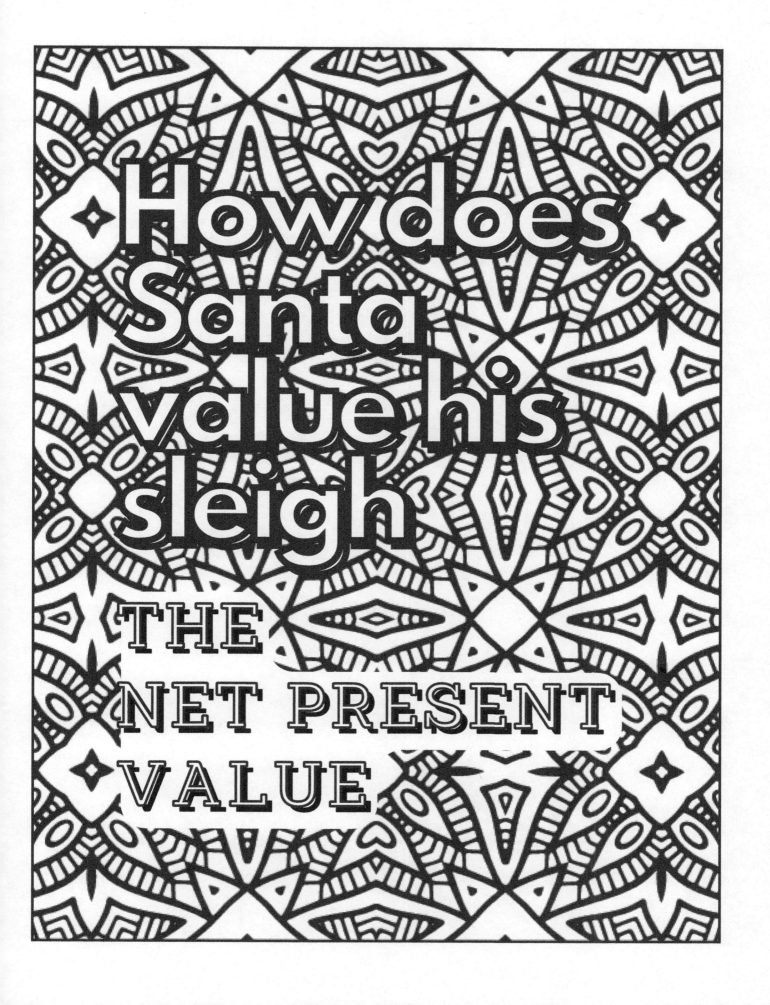

Accountants have the best

FIGURES

AND DO IT WITHOUT LOSING THEIR BALANCE

WHAT DO YOU
CALL AN
ACCOUNTANT
WITH AN
OPINION?

AN
AUDITOR

Welcome to the Accounting Department where everybody counts

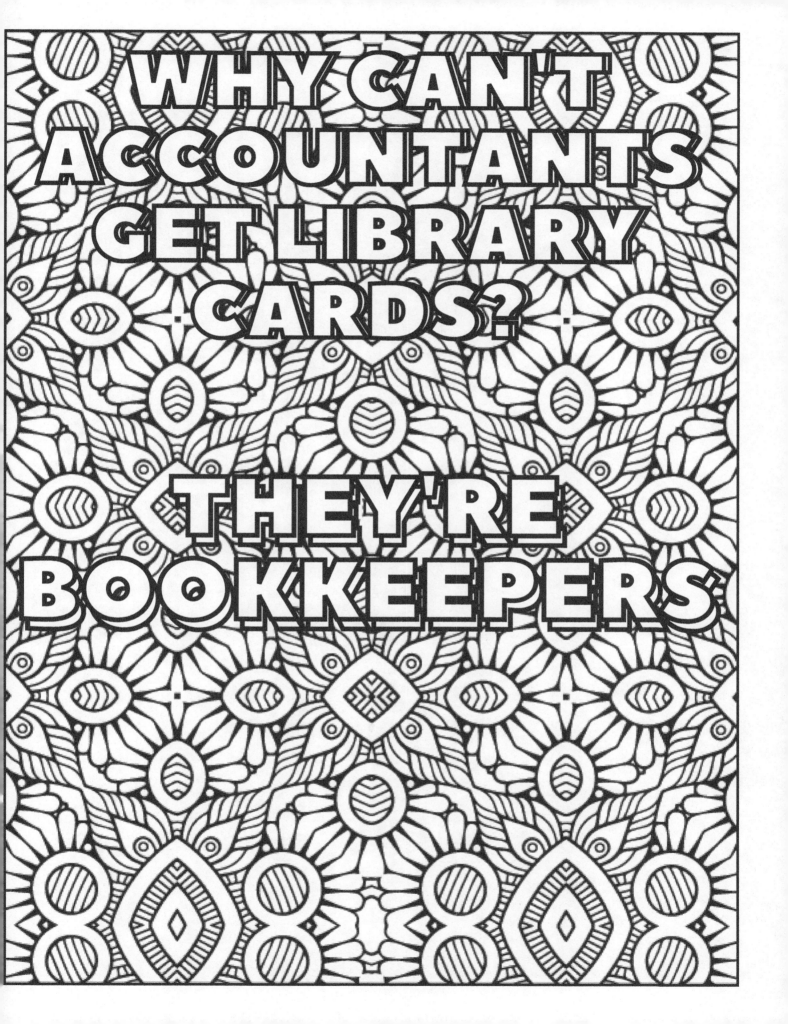

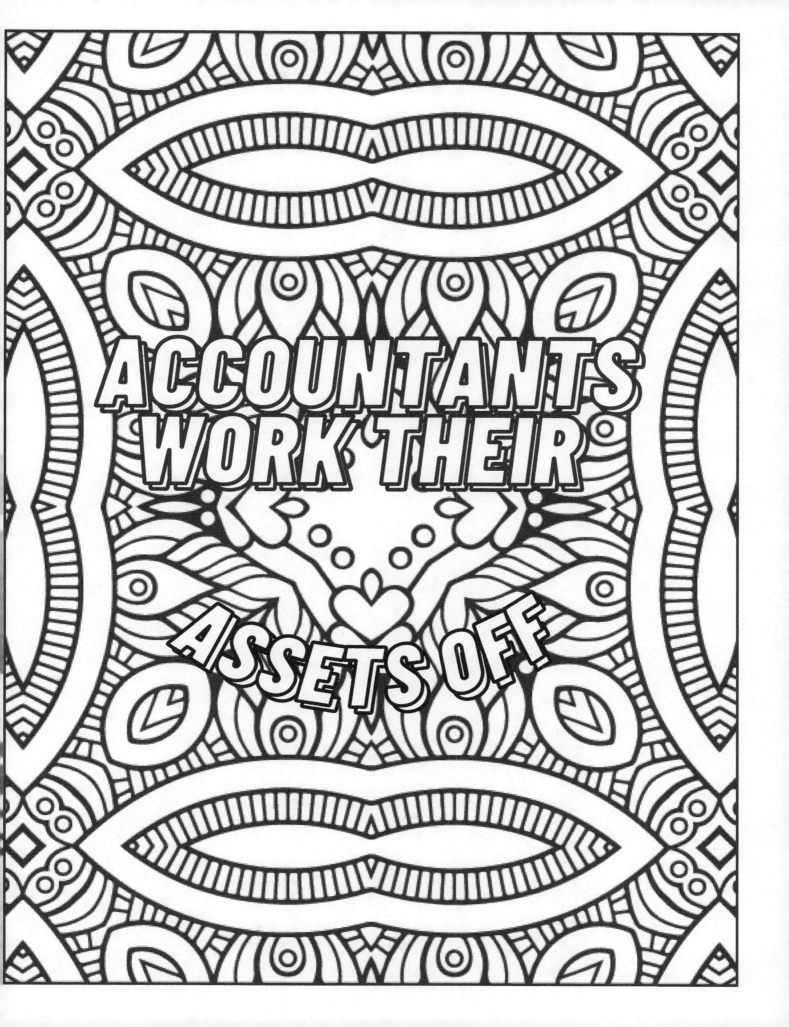

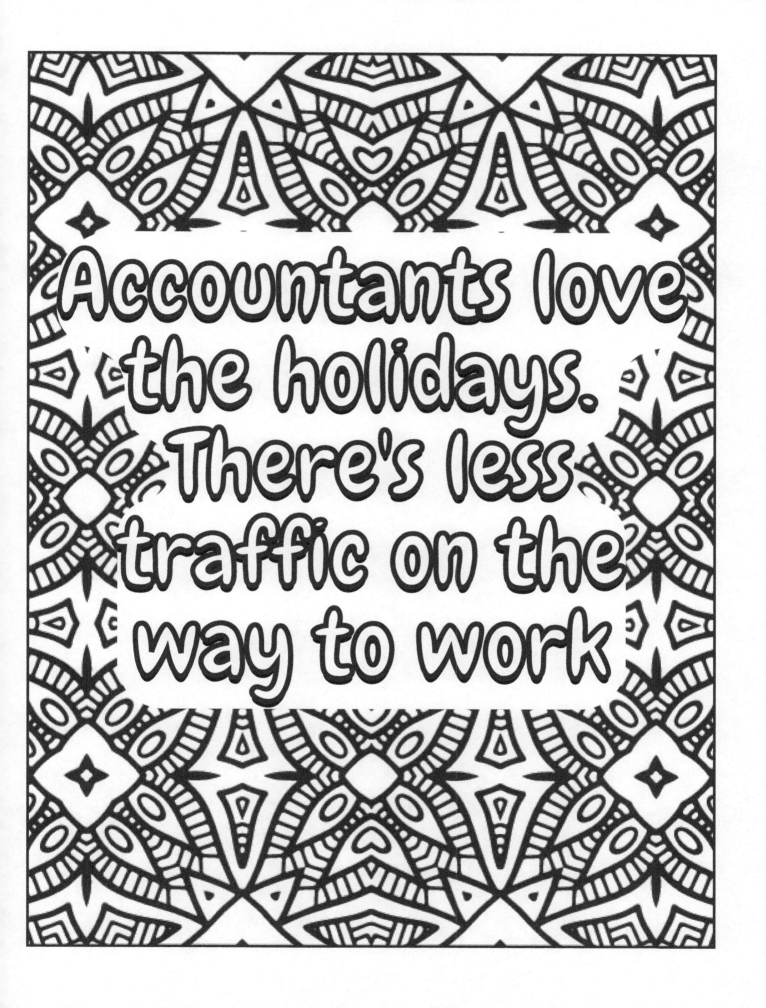

Accountants love the holidays. There's less traffic on the way to work

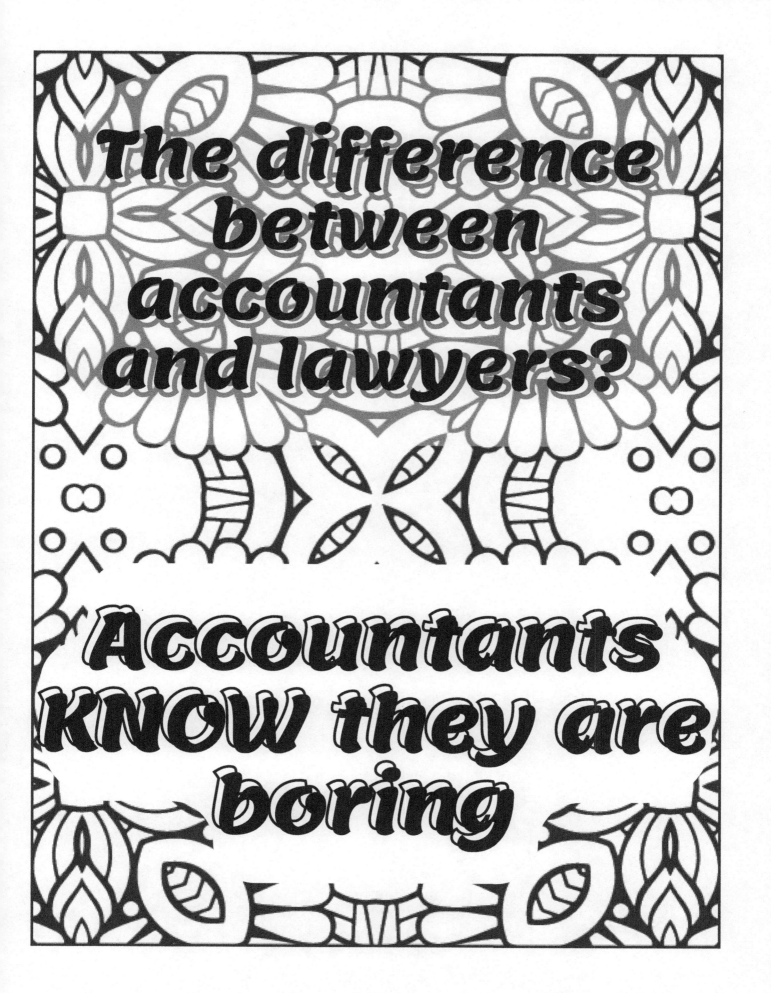

the difference between accountants and lawyers?

Accountants know they are boring

MY
ACCOUNTANT
LOVES TO SHOP
AT
THE GAP.

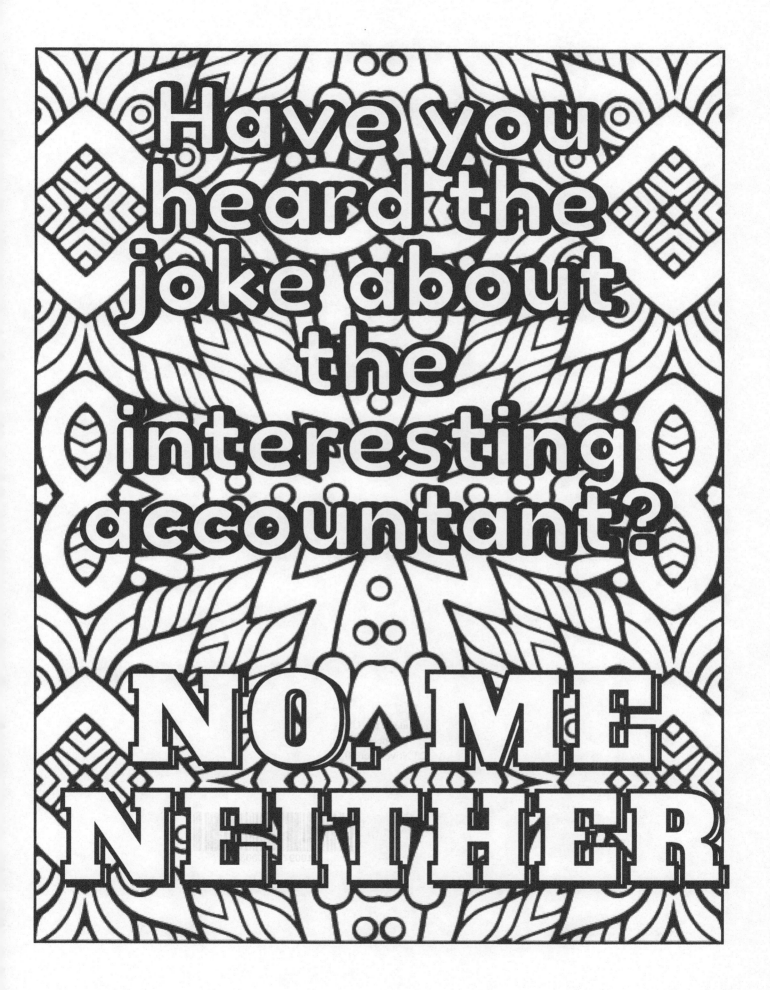

Made in the USA
Monee, IL
23 November 2024